Fact Families

Each **fact family** has the same numbers.

Giant pandas

$$\begin{array}{r} 4 \\ + 3 \\ \hline \boxed{7} \end{array} \qquad \begin{array}{r} 4 \\ + \boxed{3} \\ \hline 7 \end{array} \qquad \begin{array}{r} 7 \\ - 3 \\ \hline \boxed{4} \end{array} \qquad \begin{array}{r} \boxed{7} \\ - 4 \\ \hline 3 \end{array}$$

Fill in the missing numbers for each fact family.

1.
$$\begin{array}{r} 2 \\ + 5 \\ \hline \boxed{} \end{array} \qquad \begin{array}{r} 5 \\ + \boxed{} \\ \hline 7 \end{array} \qquad \begin{array}{r} 7 \\ - 2 \\ \hline \boxed{} \end{array} \qquad \begin{array}{r} \boxed{} \\ - 5 \\ \hline 2 \end{array}$$

2.
$$\begin{array}{r} \boxed{} \\ + 3 \\ \hline 9 \end{array} \qquad \begin{array}{r} 3 \\ + 6 \\ \hline \boxed{} \end{array} \qquad \begin{array}{r} 9 \\ - \boxed{} \\ \hline 3 \end{array} \qquad \begin{array}{r} 9 \\ - 3 \\ \hline \boxed{} \end{array}$$

3.
$$\begin{array}{r} 4 \\ + 5 \\ \hline \boxed{} \end{array} \qquad \begin{array}{r} \boxed{} \\ + 4 \\ \hline 9 \end{array} \qquad \begin{array}{r} \boxed{} \\ - 4 \\ \hline 5 \end{array} \qquad \begin{array}{r} \boxed{} \\ - 5 \\ \hline 4 \end{array}$$

4.
$$\begin{array}{r} \boxed{} \\ + 4 \\ \hline 6 \end{array} \qquad \begin{array}{r} 4 \\ + \boxed{} \\ \hline 6 \end{array} \qquad \begin{array}{r} 6 \\ - \boxed{} \\ \hline 2 \end{array} \qquad \begin{array}{r} 6 \\ - \boxed{} \\ \hline 4 \end{array}$$

5.
$$\begin{array}{r} 6 \\ + 7 \\ \hline \boxed{} \end{array} \qquad \begin{array}{r} 7 \\ + 6 \\ \hline \boxed{} \end{array} \qquad \begin{array}{r} 13 \\ - 7 \\ \hline \boxed{} \end{array} \qquad \begin{array}{r} 13 \\ - \boxed{} \\ \hline 7 \end{array}$$

6.
$$\begin{array}{r} 8 \\ + \boxed{} \\ \hline 13 \end{array} \qquad \begin{array}{r} \boxed{} \\ + 8 \\ \hline 13 \end{array} \qquad \begin{array}{r} 13 \\ - \boxed{} \\ \hline 5 \end{array} \qquad \begin{array}{r} 13 \\ - 5 \\ \hline \boxed{} \end{array}$$

7.
$$\begin{array}{r} 7 \\ + 9 \\ \hline \boxed{} \end{array} \qquad \begin{array}{r} 9 \\ + 7 \\ \hline \boxed{} \end{array} \qquad \begin{array}{r} 16 \\ - 9 \\ \hline \boxed{} \end{array} \qquad \begin{array}{r} \boxed{} \\ - 7 \\ \hline 9 \end{array}$$

8.
$$\begin{array}{r} 4 \\ + \boxed{} \\ \hline 12 \end{array} \qquad \begin{array}{r} 8 \\ + 4 \\ \hline \boxed{} \end{array} \qquad \begin{array}{r} 12 \\ - \boxed{} \\ \hline 4 \end{array} \qquad \begin{array}{r} 12 \\ - \boxed{} \\ \hline 8 \end{array}$$

Fact Families

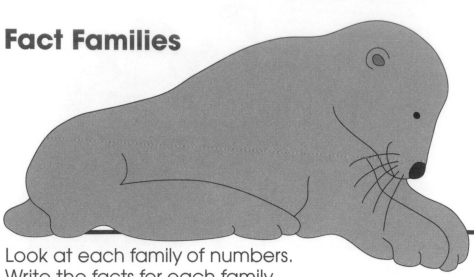

$$6, 7, 13$$
$$6 + 7 = 13$$
$$7 + 6 = 13$$
$$13 - 6 = 7$$
$$13 - 7 = 6$$

Look at each family of numbers.
Write the facts for each family.

1. **6, 8, 14**   **3, 12, 15**   **7, 8, 15**

_____   _____   _____

_____   _____   _____

_____   _____   _____

_____   _____   _____

2. **2, 18, 20**   **20, 20, 40**   **12, 13, 25**

_____   _____   _____

_____   _____   _____

_____   _____   _____

_____   _____   _____

3. **3, 5, 8**   **9, 0, 9**

_____   _____

_____   _____

_____   _____

_____   _____

Fur seals

Adding Double-Digit Numbers

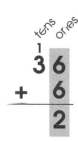

```
    tens  ones
      1
      3    6
  +        6
           2
```

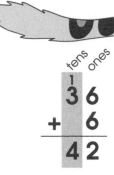

```
    tens  ones
      1
      3    6
  +        6
      4    2
```

1. Add the ones.
   6 + 6 = 12
   12 is **1** ten and **2** ones.

2. Add the tens.
   Don't forget the **1** ten.
   1 + 3 = 4 tens

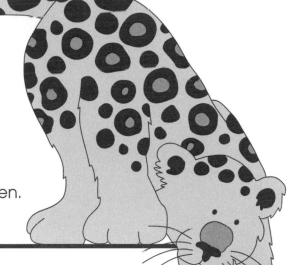

Leopards

Across

1. 55
   + 37

2. 29
   + 46

3. 47
   + 18

5. 18
   + 15

6. 59
   + 17

8. 77
   + 15

9. 25
   + 18

10. 24
    + 67

14. 14
    + 19

15. 35
    + 16

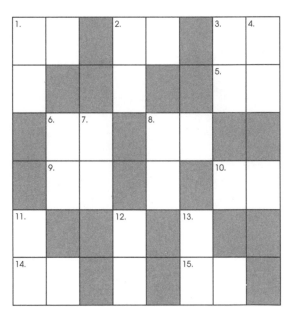

Down

1. 28
   + 68

2. 39
   + 35

3. 24
   + 39

4. 17
   + 36

6. 28
   + 46

7. 34
   + 29

8. 76
   + 14

11. 45
    + 38

12. 37
    + 58

13. 29
    + 36

Double-Digit Addition with Regrouping

Adding Three-Digit Numbers

```
  hundreds
    tens
      ones
      1
  3 4 6
+ 2 8 6
      2
```

1. Add the ones.
6 + 6 = 12
12 is 1 ten
and 2 ones.

```
  hundreds
    tens
      ones
    1 1
  3 4 6
+ 2 8 6
    3 2
```

2. Add the tens.
Don't forget
the 1 ten.
1 + 4 + 8 = 13

```
  hundreds
    tens
      ones
  1 1
  3 4 6
+ 2 8 6
  6 3 2
```

3. Add the hundreds.
Don't forget the
1 hundred.
1 + 3 + 2 = 6

Add the numbers.
Write the sums.

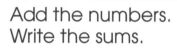

1.	221 + 579	398 + 352	375 + 246	200 + 200
2.	519 + 399	600 + 300	634 + 200	721 + 189
3.	496 + 366	100 + 500	519 + 181	131 + 689
4.	700 + 197	400 + 450	647 + 188	200 + 600

Green turtle

Leatherback
turtle

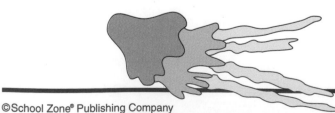

Adding Three Numbers

$$\begin{array}{r}\overset{1}{3}\;3\\8\\+1\;4\\\hline 5\end{array}$$

1. Add the ones.
   Add the first two numbers.
   $3 + 8 = 11$

   Add the third number.
   $11 + 4 = 15$

$$\begin{array}{r}\overset{1}{3}\;3\\8\\+1\;4\\\hline 5\;5\end{array}$$

2. Add the tens.
   Don't forget the **1** ten.
   $1 + 3 = 4$

   Add the third number.
   $4 + 1 = 5$

Nile crocodile

Add the numbers.
Write the sums.

1.
$$\begin{array}{r}32\\7\\+20\\\hline\end{array}\qquad\begin{array}{r}18\\1\\+36\\\hline\end{array}\qquad\begin{array}{r}21\\0\\+\;3\\\hline\end{array}\qquad\begin{array}{r}76\\2\\+11\\\hline\end{array}\qquad\begin{array}{r}2\\18\\+\;5\\\hline\end{array}$$

2.
$$\begin{array}{r}51\\5\\+\;2\\\hline\end{array}\qquad\begin{array}{r}8\\27\\+\;9\\\hline\end{array}\qquad\begin{array}{r}32\\22\\+\;5\\\hline\end{array}\qquad\begin{array}{r}56\\33\\+10\\\hline\end{array}\qquad\begin{array}{r}35\\42\\+\;5\\\hline\end{array}$$

3.
$$\begin{array}{r}3\\21\\+\;5\\\hline\end{array}\qquad\begin{array}{r}25\\46\\+14\\\hline\end{array}\qquad\begin{array}{r}6\\2\\+54\\\hline\end{array}\qquad\begin{array}{r}62\\33\\+\;5\\\hline\end{array}\qquad\begin{array}{r}83\\5\\+20\\\hline\end{array}$$

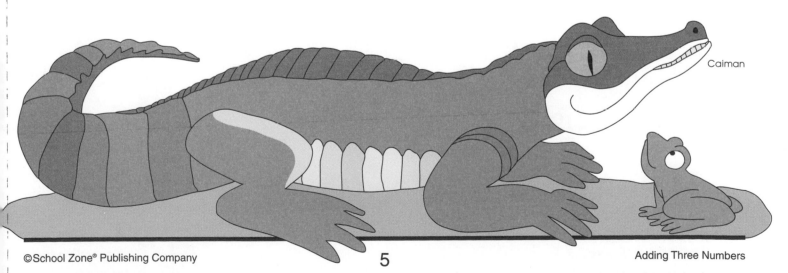

Caiman

Writing Numbers in Order

Vino snake

Fruit bat

Read each set of numbers.
Write them in order from the least to the greatest.

1. **36, 19, 47, 21** _____ _____ _____ _____

2. **76, 65, 33, 56** _____ _____ _____ _____

3. **59, 46, 32, 17** _____ _____ _____ _____

4. **89, 26, 39, 19** _____ _____ _____ _____

5. **319, 721, 976, 351** _____ _____ _____ _____

6. **572, 897, 711, 999** _____ _____ _____ _____

7. **702, 124, 231, 100** _____ _____ _____ _____

8. **308, 788, 416, 596** _____ _____ _____ _____

9. **102, 36, 98, 419** _____ _____ _____ _____

10. **42, 813, 56, 789** _____ _____ _____ _____

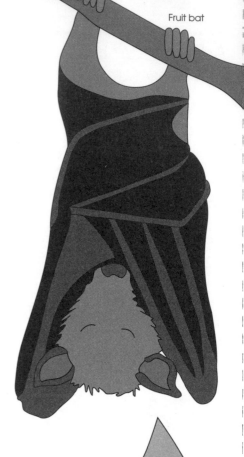

Ordering Numbers

Subtracting Double-Digit Numbers

```
tens ones
  3 4
 -1 7
```

1. Start with the ones.
   4 – 7 cannot be done.
   You must rename.

```
  2 14
  3 4
 -1 7
```

2. Take **1** ten from the tens.
   10 + 4 = 14 in the ones.
   3 – 1 = 2 in the tens.

```
  2 14
  3 4
 -1 7
  1 7
```

3. Now subtract.
   Ones first.
   Now the tens.

Subtract the numbers.
Write each difference.
Rename if needed.

1.
```
  65
 -22
```
```
  28
 -13
```
```
  63
 -24
```
```
  96
 -35
```

2.
```
  86
 -85
```
```
  78
 -33
```
```
  36
 -28
```
```
  77
 -35
```

3.
```
  80
 -31
```
```
  92
 -54
```
```
  67
 -18
```
```
  36
 -27
```

4.
```
  99
 -44
```
```
  85
 -49
```
```
  82
 -55
```
```
  90
 -25
```

Ostriches

Subtracting Three-Digit Numbers

1. Subtract the ones.
   8 – 9 cannot be done.
   Rename **8** to **18** and
   then subtract.

2. Subtract the tens.
   Remember the **1** is gone.
   0 – 0 = 0

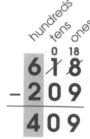

3. Subtract the hundreds.
   6 – 2 = 4

Subtract the numbers.
Write each difference.
Rename if needed.

Sea otters

1.
```
  148        174        243        255
-  36      -  43      -  33      -  48
```

2.
```
  353        326        870        258
- 205      - 250      - 328      - 146
```

3.
```
  694        786        971        777
- 589      - 579      -  26      - 456
```

4.
```
  219        493        800        550
-  14      - 188      - 250      - 315
```

Three-Digit Subtraction

Let's Expand

Write the following number in expanded notation using numerals.

372 = 300 + 70 + 2

Write the number in expanded notation using words this time.

372 = **3** hundreds + **7** tens + **2** ones

Write the following numbers in expanded notation using numerals.

1. **562** = _____ + _____ + _____

2. **953** = _____ + _____ + _____

3. **375** = _____ + _____ + _____

4. **617** = _____ + _____ + _____

5. **109** = _____ + _____ + _____

Polar bears

Write the following numbers in expanded notation using words.

6. **749** = _____ + _____ + _____

7. **514** = _____ + _____ + _____

8. **936** = _____ + _____ + _____

9. **398** = _____ + _____ + _____

10. **617** = _____ + _____ + _____

Find Thousands, Hundreds, Tens, and Ones

	7	**8**	**3**	**4**
7,834	thousands	hundreds	tens	ones

In each number below, one digit is in boldface.
Circle the answer that shows the place value of that digit.
The first answer is circled for you.

1. 2,43**5**   thousands   hundreds   tens   (ones)

2. 8,**2**59   thousands   hundreds   tens   ones

3. **1**,020   thousands   hundreds   tens   ones

4. **2**,435   thousands   hundreds   tens   ones

5. 9,5**4**1   thousands   hundreds   tens   ones

6. 1,02**0**   thousands   hundreds   tens   ones

Circle the correct digits. The first answer is circled for you.

7. Circle the ones.   8 , 1 9 (1)

8. Circle the thousands.   4 , 2 7 5

9. Circle the hundreds.   1 , 2 4 3

10. Circle the tens.   9 , 4 7 0

11. Circle the thousands.   5 , 4 3 7

12. Circle the hundreds.   7 , 7 5 1

Cheetahs

Place Value: 1,000s, 100s, 10s, and 1s

Place Value

Across

1. **2** hundreds + **6** tens + **8** ones
3. **3** hundreds + **9** tens + **7** ones
5. **4** thousands + **7** hundreds + **8** tens + **0** ones
7. three thousand three hundred thirty-three
8. **200** less than **9235**
9. six hundred twenty-two
11. **6** hundreds + **7** tens + **8** ones
13. **500** less than **5890**
15. **8** thousands + **1** hundred + **2** tens + **6** ones
16. **70** more than **120**
17. two thousand five hundred fifty

(Check your answers with the down numbers.)

Down

1. **2** thousands + **9** hundreds + **5** tens + **9** ones
2. eight thousand four hundred thirty-three
3. **2000** more than **1036**
4. **7** thousands + **3** hundreds + **9** tens + **2** ones
6. **1000** less than **8354**
10. two thousand five hundred ninety-nine
11. **10** less than **695**
12. **400** more than **422**
14. **3** hundreds + **1** ten + **0** ones

Galápagos penguins

Place Value: 1,000s, 100s, 10s, and 1s

Greater or Less Than

Brown pelicans

1,525 is greater than **1,520**.

1,52_5_ > 1,52_0_

Which digits did you compare? ___ones___

2,650 is less than **3,210**.

_2_,650 < _3_,210

Which digits did you compare? _thousands_

Place a **>** or **<** in each circle.

1. **5,148** ◯ **4,185**   Which digits did you compare? _____
2. **6,450** ◯ **6,504**   Which digits did you compare? _____
3. **5,709** ◯ **5,704**   Which digits did you compare? _____
4. **9,205** ◯ **9,250**   Which digits did you compare? _____
5. **3,239** ◯ **3,299**   Which digits did you compare? _____
6. **4,398** ◯ **2,459**   Which digits did you compare? _____
7. **2,879** ◯ **2,814**   Which digits did you compare? _____

Write these numbers in order from least to greatest.

8. **6,705 6,075 6,507 675**   ____ ____ ____ ____

9. **4,279 7,942 987 4,297**   ____ ____ ____ ____

10. **56 506 6,052 6,502**   ____ ____ ____ ____

Challenge: Use the digits **3, 9, 1, 6** to write the greatest four-digit number you can. _____

Adding Four-Digit Numbers

```
        ones            tens          hundreds      thousands
     1                1 1           1 1           1 1
  7,286           7,286          7,286          7,286
+ 2,465         + 2,465        + 2,465        + 2,465
───────         ───────        ───────        ───────
      1              51            751          9,751
```

Start with the ones. Then move to the tens.
Go on to the hundreds. Finally, add the thousands.
Put a comma between the hundreds and thousands place.

Find the sum for each problem. Place a comma in your answer.
Remember: you may need to regroup more than once in a problem.

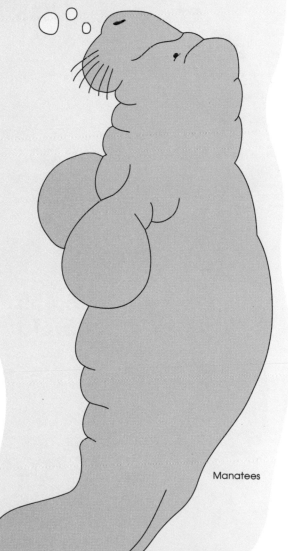

1. $\begin{array}{r} 4,840 \\ + 1,023 \\ \hline \end{array}$ $\begin{array}{r} 5,462 \\ + 923 \\ \hline \end{array}$ $\begin{array}{r} 2,640 \\ + 3,173 \\ \hline \end{array}$

2. $\begin{array}{r} 8,540 \\ + 482 \\ \hline \end{array}$ $\begin{array}{r} 7,731 \\ + 1,273 \\ \hline \end{array}$ $\begin{array}{r} 1,847 \\ + 6,259 \\ \hline \end{array}$

3. $\begin{array}{r} 4,787 \\ + 1,896 \\ \hline \end{array}$ $\begin{array}{r} 6,354 \\ + 2,498 \\ \hline \end{array}$ $\begin{array}{r} 2,743 \\ + 5,189 \\ \hline \end{array}$

4. $\begin{array}{r} 3,086 \\ + 5,027 \\ \hline \end{array}$ $\begin{array}{r} 6,259 \\ + 1,362 \\ \hline \end{array}$ $\begin{array}{r} 4,274 \\ + 3,899 \\ \hline \end{array}$

Manatees

Subtracting Four-Digit Numbers

```
      ones              tens              hundreds
                                           1  16
   2,6 3 7           2,6 3 7           2,6 3 7
 - 1,7 1 5         - 1,7 1 5         - 1,7 1 5
         2              2 2            9 2 2
```

Remember: Start with the ones.

Find the difference for each problem.
Place a comma in your answer if it has 4 digits.
Remember: you may need to rename more than once in a problem.

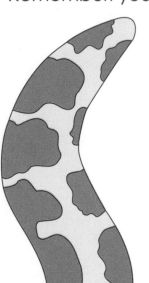

1.
$$\begin{array}{r} 4,345 \\ -\ 3,261 \\ \hline \end{array}$$
$$\begin{array}{r} 3,926 \\ -2,842 \\ \hline \end{array}$$
$$\begin{array}{r} 1,135 \\ -\ \ 841 \\ \hline \end{array}$$

2.
$$\begin{array}{r} 9,004 \\ -\ 7,539 \\ \hline \end{array}$$
$$\begin{array}{r} 6,757 \\ -4,902 \\ \hline \end{array}$$
$$\begin{array}{r} 3,502 \\ -\ 1,201 \\ \hline \end{array}$$

3.
$$\begin{array}{r} 8,435 \\ -\ 5,713 \\ \hline \end{array}$$
$$\begin{array}{r} 6,005 \\ -2,076 \\ \hline \end{array}$$
$$\begin{array}{r} 5,806 \\ -3,402 \\ \hline \end{array}$$

4.
$$\begin{array}{r} 4,200 \\ -\ \ 374 \\ \hline \end{array}$$
$$\begin{array}{r} 7,261 \\ -3,521 \\ \hline \end{array}$$
$$\begin{array}{r} 9,214 \\ -7,007 \\ \hline \end{array}$$

Indian python

Let's Learn About Rounding

Rounding means making a number smaller or larger.
To round to the nearest ten, look at the ones place.
If the number is **5** or more, round up to the nearest ten.
If the number is **4** or less, round down to the nearest ten.

90
89
88
87
86
85
84
83
82
81
80

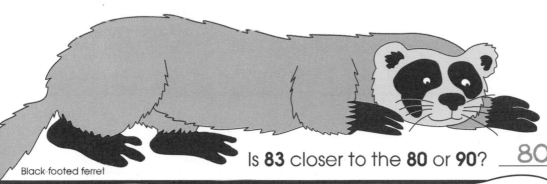

Black-footed ferret

Is **83** closer to the **80** or **90**? _80_

Look at each number in bold face below.
Circle the number that rounds to the nearest ten.
The first one is circled for you.

1. **32**	(30)	40	2. **89**	80	90
19	10	20	**64**	60	70
55	50	60	**26**	20	30
41	40	50	**77**	70	80
28	20	30	**39**	30	40
62	60	70	**33**	30	40

Round each number to the nearest ten. The first one
is done for you.

3. **64**	_60_	4. **86**	____
22	____	**49**	____
31	____	**43**	____
35	____	**67**	____
18	____	**3**	____
89	____	**76**	____

Mexican
prairie dogs

Multiplying Sets

This is a set of **2** bears.

Here are **3** sets with **2** bears in each one.

   **3 x 2 = 6**
6 is the **product**.

Brown bear

Multiply the numbers.
Write the products.

1. **2 x 4 =** _____

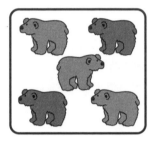 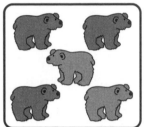

2 x 5 = _____

2. **2 x 6 =** _____

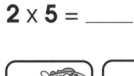  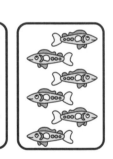

3 x 6 = _____

3. **2 x 8 =** _____

2 x 7 = _____

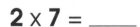

Multiplying by 0, 1, 2, and 3

Multiplication is **repeated addition**.

$3 \times 5 = 15$ is $5 + 5 + 5 = 15$

$3 \times 5 =$ ___15___

Multiply the numbers. Write the products.

Count by **2**s.

1. $2 \times 2 =$ _____

$2 \times 3 =$ _____

$2 \times 4 =$ _____

$2 \times 5 =$ _____

$2 \times 6 =$ _____

$2 \times 7 =$ _____

$2 \times 8 =$ _____

$2 \times 9 =$ _____

Count by **3**s.

2. $3 \times 2 =$ _____

$3 \times 3 =$ _____

$3 \times 4 =$ _____

$3 \times 5 =$ _____

$3 \times 6 =$ _____

$3 \times 7 =$ _____

$3 \times 8 =$ _____

$3 \times 9 =$ _____

Any number times **1** equals that number.
Any number times **0** equals **0**.
Multiply the numbers. Write the products.

3. $1 \times 2 =$ _____

$1 \times 1 =$ _____

$1 \times 3 =$ _____

$4 \times 1 =$ _____

$1 \times 6 =$ _____

$5 \times 1 =$ _____

$7 \times 1 =$ _____

$1 \times 8 =$ _____

4. $3 \times 0 =$ _____

$0 \times 2 =$ _____

$0 \times 4 =$ _____

$6 \times 0 =$ _____

$5 \times 0 =$ _____

$0 \times 9 =$ _____

$0 \times 8 =$ _____

$0 \times 1 =$ _____

Whooping cranes

More Multiplying

Number order does not matter in multiplication. **4** x **2** is the same as **2** x **4**.

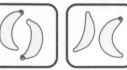 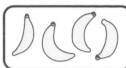

Multiply the numbers. Write the products.

Count by **4**s.   Count by **5**s.

1. **4** x **2** = _____   2. **5** x **2** = _____
    4 x **3** = _____   **5** x **3** = _____
    4 x **4** = _____   **5** x **4** = _____
    4 x **5** = _____   **5** x **5** = _____
    4 x **6** = _____   **5** x **6** = _____
    4 x **7** = _____   **5** x **7** = _____
    4 x **8** = _____   **5** x **8** = _____
    4 x **9** = _____   **5** x **9** = _____

Practice these facts.
Write the products.

3. **4** x **5** = _____   4. **8** x **0** = _____
    3 x **3** = _____   **5** x **4** = _____
    5 x **7** = _____   **3** x **7** = _____
    5 x **1** = _____   **4** x **8** = _____
    3 x **6** = _____   **5** x **9** = _____
    2 x **7** = _____   **2** x **5** = _____
    4 x **3** = _____   **4** x **4** = _____
    2 x **9** = _____   **4** x **7** = _____

Chimpanzee

More Multiplying

Across

1. 5 × 2

2. 8 × 3

3. 5 × 6

4. 4 × 3

5. 8 × 2

6. 7 × 5

7. 6 × 2

8. 2 × 9

9. 8 × 5

10. 5 × 5

11. 3 × 7

12. 8 × 3

Down

1. 7 × 2

2. 5 × 4

3. 8 × 4

4. 4 × 4

5. 5 × 3

6. 4 × 8

7. 6 × 3

8. 2 × 5

9. 9 × 5

10. 7 × 3

11. 4 × 6

12. 7 × 4

Dividing by 2

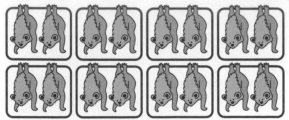

There are __8__ sets of two in **16**. **16 ÷ 2 =** __8__

8 is the **quotient**.

Townsend's big-eared bat

Divide the numbers. Write the quotients.

1. There are _____ sets of two in **4**.

    4 ÷ 2 = ____

There are _____ sets of two in **6**.

6 ÷ 2 = ____

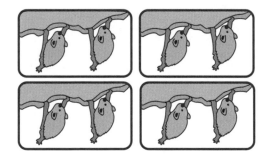

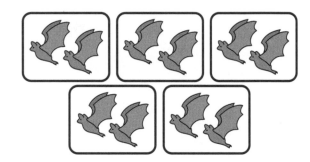

2. There are _____ sets of two in **8**.

    8 ÷ 2 = ____

There are _____ sets of two in **10**.

10 ÷ 2 = ____

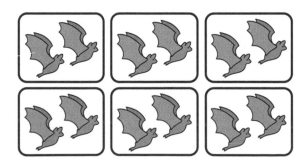

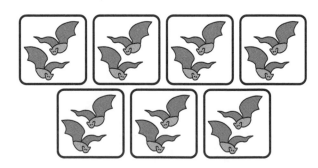

3. There are _____ sets of two in **12**.

    12 ÷ 2 = ____

There are _____ sets of two in **14**.

14 ÷ 2 = ____

Dividing by 3

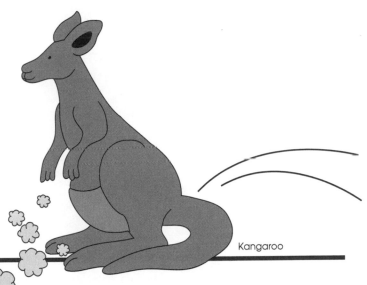

Kangaroo

There are __8__ sets of three in **24**.

24 ÷ 3 = __8__

Divide the numbers. Write the quotients.

1. There are _____ sets of three in **6**.

    6 ÷ 3 = _____

    There are _____ sets of three in **9**.

    9 ÷ 3 = _____

2. There are _____ sets of three in **12**.

    12 ÷ 3 = _____

    There are _____ sets of three in **15**.

    15 ÷ 3 = _____

3. There are _____ sets of three in **18**.

    18 ÷ 3 = _____

    There are _____ sets of three in **21**.

    21 ÷ 3 = _____

21

Dividing by 3

Fact Families

If you know your multiplication facts, you are ready for division.

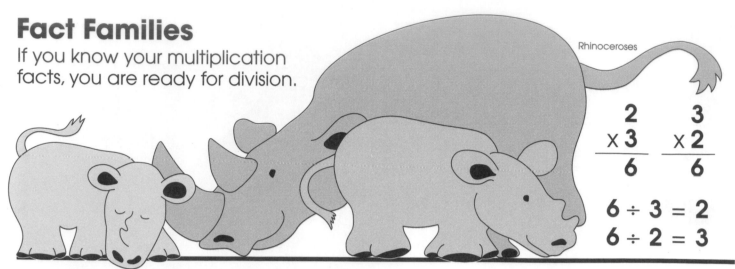

Rhinoceroses

$$\begin{array}{r} 2 \\ \times\ 3 \\ \hline 6 \end{array} \qquad \begin{array}{r} 3 \\ \times\ 2 \\ \hline 6 \end{array}$$

$6 \div 3 = 2$

$6 \div 2 = 3$

Fill in the missing numbers for each fact family.

1.
$$\begin{array}{r} 2 \\ \times\ 4 \\ \hline \boxed{} \end{array} \qquad \begin{array}{r} 4 \\ \times\ \boxed{} \\ \hline 8 \end{array}$$

$8 \div 2 = \boxed{}$

$8 \div \boxed{} = 2$

2.
$$\begin{array}{r} 3 \\ \times\ 5 \\ \hline \boxed{} \end{array} \qquad \begin{array}{r} 5 \\ \times\ \boxed{} \\ \hline 15 \end{array}$$

$15 \div 5 = \boxed{}$

$15 \div \boxed{} = 5$

3.
$$\begin{array}{r} 2 \\ \times\ \boxed{} \\ \hline 14 \end{array} \qquad \begin{array}{r} 7 \\ \times\ \boxed{} \\ \hline 14 \end{array}$$

$\boxed{} \div 2 = 7$

$14 \div \boxed{} = 2$

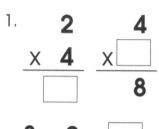

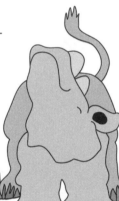

4.
$$\begin{array}{r} \boxed{} \\ \times\ 3 \\ \hline 24 \end{array} \qquad \begin{array}{r} 8 \\ \times\ \boxed{} \\ \hline 24 \end{array}$$

$24 \div \boxed{} = 8$

$24 \div \boxed{} = 3$

5.
$$\begin{array}{r} 5 \\ \times\ \boxed{} \\ \hline 30 \end{array} \qquad \begin{array}{r} 6 \\ \times\ 5 \\ \hline \boxed{} \end{array}$$

$30 \div \boxed{} = 6$

$30 \div 6 = \boxed{}$

6.
$$\begin{array}{r} 4 \\ \times\ 7 \\ \hline \boxed{} \end{array} \qquad \begin{array}{r} \boxed{} \\ \times\ 4 \\ \hline 28 \end{array}$$

$28 \div \boxed{} = 4$

$\boxed{} \div 4 = 7$

Rewrite these multiplication facts as division facts.

7. $\quad 4 \times 3 = 12 \qquad\qquad\qquad 6 \times 3 = 18 \qquad\qquad\qquad 3 \times 7 = 21$

_____ ÷ _____ = _____   _____ ÷ _____ = _____   _____ ÷ _____ = _____

_____ ÷ _____ = _____   _____ ÷ _____ = _____   _____ ÷ _____ = _____

Dividing by 4 and 5

Sockeye salmon

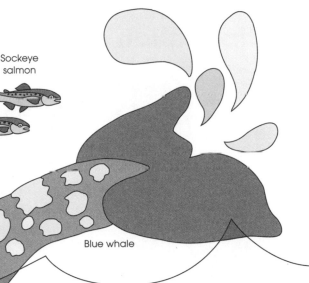

Blue whale

Circle the fish to show **15 ÷ 5**.

How many groups of 5? _____

Divide the numbers.
Write the quotients.

1. **8 ÷ 4 =** _____
   12 ÷ 4 = _____
   16 ÷ 4 = _____
   20 ÷ 4 = _____
   24 ÷ 4 = _____
   28 ÷ 4 = _____
   32 ÷ 4 = _____
   36 ÷ 4 = _____

2. **10 ÷ 5 =** _____
   15 ÷ 5 = _____
   20 ÷ 5 = _____
   25 ÷ 5 = _____
   30 ÷ 5 = _____
   35 ÷ 5 = _____
   40 ÷ 5 = _____
   45 ÷ 5 = _____

Practice the facts.

3. **6 ÷ 3 =** _____
   10 ÷ 2 = _____
   20 ÷ 4 = _____
   20 ÷ 5 = _____
   25 ÷ 5 = _____
   8 ÷ 4 = _____
   16 ÷ 4 = _____
   21 ÷ 3 = _____

4. **4 ÷ 2 =** _____
   15 ÷ 5 = _____
   20 ÷ 2 = _____
   12 ÷ 3 = _____
   18 ÷ 2 = _____
   10 ÷ 5 = _____
   12 ÷ 2 = _____
   28 ÷ 4 = _____

Division

Multiplication and Division

Spectacled bear

0⟍24 Dividing by zero has no meaning.

Read each problem.
Write the product or quotient. (Remember: we never divide by 0.)

1.
$$\begin{array}{r} 2 \\ \times\,2 \\ \hline \end{array}$$
$$\begin{array}{r} 9 \\ \times\,0 \\ \hline \end{array}$$
$$\begin{array}{r} 5 \\ \times\,9 \\ \hline \end{array}$$
$$\begin{array}{r} 4 \\ \times\,8 \\ \hline \end{array}$$
$$\begin{array}{r} 5 \\ \times\,6 \\ \hline \end{array}$$

2.   2⟌14   4⟌24   4⟌12   3⟌21   5⟌40

3.
$$\begin{array}{r} 5 \\ \times\,7 \\ \hline \end{array}$$
$$\begin{array}{r} 4 \\ \times\,4 \\ \hline \end{array}$$
$$\begin{array}{r} 2 \\ \times\,9 \\ \hline \end{array}$$
$$\begin{array}{r} 5 \\ \times\,1 \\ \hline \end{array}$$
$$\begin{array}{r} 3 \\ \times\,9 \\ \hline \end{array}$$

4.   3⟌9   5⟌35   4⟌8   4⟌36   4⟌16

Carla wants to buy animal stamps. She
has **28** cents. Each stamp costs **7** cents.
How many stamps can she buy? _____

Multiplication

Boutu

Remember: multiplication is repeated addition.

Multiply the numbers. Write the products.
Count by **6**s.

1. **6 x 2** = _____

   6 x 3 = _____

   6 x 4 = _____

   6 x 5 = _____

   6 x 6 = _____

   6 x 7 = _____

   6 x 8 = _____

   6 x 9 = _____

Count by **7**s.

2. **7 x 2** = _____

   7 x 3 = _____

   7 x 4 = _____

   7 x 5 = _____

   7 x 6 = _____

   7 x 7 = _____

   7 x 8 = _____

   7 x 9 = _____

Practice these facts.
Write the products.
Count by **8**s.

3. **8 x 2** = _____

   8 x 3 = _____

   8 x 4 = _____

   8 x 5 = _____

   8 x 6 = _____

   8 x 7 = _____

   8 x 8 = _____

   8 x 9 = _____

When the number **9** is multiplied by
a single digit, the product always
adds up to **9**. Count by **9**s.

4. **9 x 2** = _18_   **1 + 8** = _9_

   9 x 3 = _____   **2 + 7** = _____

   9 x 4 = _____   **3 + 6** = _____

   9 x 5 = _____   **4 + 5** = _____

   9 x 6 = _____   **5 + 4** = _____

   9 x 7 = _____   **6 + 3** = _____

   9 x 8 = _____   **7 + 2** = _____

   9 x 9 = _____   **8 + 1** = _____

Multiplying Two-Digit Numbers by One Digit

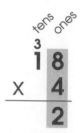

$$\begin{array}{r} \overset{3}{1}\,8 \\ \times\ \ 4 \\ \hline 2 \end{array}$$

$$\begin{array}{r} \overset{3}{1}\,8 \\ \times\ \ 4 \\ \hline 7\,2 \end{array}$$

1. Multiply the ones.
   4 x 8 = 32
   Regroup the **3** tens.

2. Multiply the tens.
   4 x 1 = 4
   4 tens + **3** tens = **7** tens

African elephants

Find the product for each problem.

1.
$$\begin{array}{r} 29 \\ \times\ 3 \end{array}$$
$$\begin{array}{r} 12 \\ \times\ 6 \end{array}$$
$$\begin{array}{r} 24 \\ \times\ 8 \end{array}$$
$$\begin{array}{r} 13 \\ \times\ 4 \end{array}$$

2.
$$\begin{array}{r} 16 \\ \times\ 4 \end{array}$$
$$\begin{array}{r} 33 \\ \times\ 5 \end{array}$$
$$\begin{array}{r} 36 \\ \times\ 3 \end{array}$$
$$\begin{array}{r} 18 \\ \times\ 2 \end{array}$$

3.
$$\begin{array}{r} 61 \\ \times\ 8 \end{array}$$
$$\begin{array}{r} 52 \\ \times\ 7 \end{array}$$
$$\begin{array}{r} 47 \\ \times\ 3 \end{array}$$
$$\begin{array}{r} 91 \\ \times\ 9 \end{array}$$

4.
$$\begin{array}{r} 98 \\ \times\ 2 \end{array}$$
$$\begin{array}{r} 34 \\ \times\ 8 \end{array}$$
$$\begin{array}{r} 40 \\ \times\ 6 \end{array}$$
$$\begin{array}{r} 14 \\ \times\ 7 \end{array}$$

Multiplying Three-Digit Numbers by One Digit

$$
\begin{array}{r}
1\ 2\ \overset{3}{8} \\
\times\quad 4 \\
\hline
2
\end{array}
$$

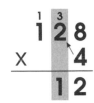
$$
\begin{array}{r}
1\ \overset{3}{2}\ 8 \\
\times\quad 4 \\
\hline
1\ 2
\end{array}
$$

$$
\begin{array}{r}
\overset{1}{1}\ \overset{3}{2}\ 8 \\
\times\quad 4 \\
\hline
5\ 1\ 2
\end{array}
$$

1. Multiply the ones.
   4 x 8 = 32
   Regroup the **3** tens.

2. Multiply the tens.
   8 tens + **3** tens = **11** tens
   Regroup the **1** hundred.

3. Multiply the hundreds.
   4 hundreds + **1** hundred = **5** hundreds

Multiply to find the product in each problem.
Then find the products in the number search puzzle.

1.
$$
\begin{array}{r} 318 \\ \times\ \ 3 \\ \hline \end{array}
\qquad
\begin{array}{r} 164 \\ \times\ \ 5 \\ \hline \end{array}
\qquad
\begin{array}{r} 408 \\ \times\ \ 6 \\ \hline \end{array}
$$

2.
$$
\begin{array}{r} 237 \\ \times\ \ 8 \\ \hline \end{array}
\qquad
\begin{array}{r} 128 \\ \times\ \ 2 \\ \hline \end{array}
\qquad
\begin{array}{r} 333 \\ \times\ \ 7 \\ \hline \end{array}
$$

3.
$$
\begin{array}{r} 350 \\ \times\ \ 2 \\ \hline \end{array}
\qquad
\begin{array}{r} 508 \\ \times\ \ 4 \\ \hline \end{array}
\qquad
\begin{array}{r} 143 \\ \times\ \ 6 \\ \hline \end{array}
$$

Mountain gorillas

8	2	8	5	8	7	9
5	2	7	1	2	1	3
0	1	0	3	8	5	2
2	3	0	4	4	9	5
8	2	4	4	2	5	6
0	2	3	3	1	4	7

Multiplication Clue Words

Some words often mean to multiply. Some multiplication clue words are **how many** and **how much**. When you multiply, you are adding numbers.

A cheetah can cover as many as **20** feet in one stride. How many feet can it cover in **6** strides?

1. Read the problem carefully.
2. Look for clue words.
3. Decide what you must do.
4. Solve the problem.

$$\begin{array}{r} 20 \\ \times\ \ 6 \\ \hline 120 \end{array}$$

The cheetah can cover **120** feet in **6** strides.

Solve the problems.

1. If a gibbon can cover **12** feet in a single swing through the trees, how many feet can it cover in **9** swings? _____

2. An elephant in the wild needs about **400** pounds of food a day. How many pounds of food does it need in **7** days? _____

3. A grizzly bear may eat **85** pounds of fish, grasses, and leaves a day during the summer and fall. How many pounds of food will it eat in **8** days? _____

Division Clue Words

Division does not have many clue words. Most of the time **how many** is used. And most of the time the word **each** Is used. When you divide, you are separating something into equal parts.

20 fish
4 groups
How many fish in each group?

1. Read the problem carefully.
2. Look for clue words.
3. Decide what you must do.
4. Solve the problem.

$$4 \overline{) 20}$$

```
      5
4 ) 20
    20
  ----
     0
```

There are **5** fish in each group.

Solve the problems.

Asiatic lions

1. **21** birds
   7 cages
   How many birds in each cage? _____

2. **45** loaves of bread
   9 elephants
   How many loaves for each elephant? _____

3. **30** bananas
   6 monkeys
   How many bananas for each monkey? _____

4. **63** lions
   9 lions in each group
   How many groups of lions? _____

Division Clue Words

Division Story Problems

Mrs. Smith's class is going on a field trip to the zoo. There are **20** students in the class. The school vans can each carry **5** students. How many vans are needed?

1. Read the problem carefully.
2. Look for clue words.
3. Decide what you must do.
4. Solve the problem.

$$5\overline{)20} = 4 \text{ vans}$$
$$\underline{20}$$
$$0$$

Solve the problems.

1. There are **24** pounds of fish. There are **8** seals to feed. How many pounds of fish for each seal?   _____

2. Shana has **18** animal cards. She wants to give them to **3** friends. How many animal cards will each friend get?   _____

3. The school library has **42** books about animals. A group of **6** students is reading the books for a project. How many books will each student read?   _____

4. A chimpanzee usually has a baby every **4** years. How many babies could she have in **28** years?   _____

Division Story Problems

Answer Key

Page 1
1. 7, 2, 5, 7
2. 6, 9, 6, 6
3. 9, 5, 9, 9
4. 2, 2, 4, 2
5. 13, 13, 6, 6
6. 5, 5, 8, 8
7. 16, 16, 7, 16
8. 8, 12, 8, 4

Page 4
1. 800, 750, 621, 400
2. 918, 900, 834, 910
3. 862, 600, 700, 820
4. 897, 850, 835, 800

Page 2
1.
6 + 8 = 14	3 + 12 = 15	7 + 8 = 15
8 + 6 = 14	12 + 3 = 15	8 + 7 = 15
14 – 6 = 8	15 – 3 = 12	15 – 7 = 8
14 – 8 = 6	15 – 12 = 3	15 – 8 = 7

2.
2 + 18 = 20	20 + 20 = 40	12 + 13 = 25
18 + 2 = 20	20 + 20 = 40	13 + 12 = 25
20 – 2 = 18	40 – 20 = 20	25 – 12 = 13
20 – 18 = 2	40 – 20 = 20	25 – 13 = 12

3.
3 + 5 = 8	9 + 0 = 9
5 + 3 = 8	0 + 9 = 9
8 – 3 = 5	9 – 0 = 9
8 – 5 = 3	

Page 3

(crossword-style number grid)
9	2		7	5		6	5
6				4		3	3
		7	6		9	2	
	4	3		0		9	1
8				9		6	
3	3		3	5		5	1

Page 5
1. 59, 55, 24, 89, 25
2. 58, 44, 59, 99, 82
3. 29, 85, 62, 100, 108

Page 6
1. 19, 21, 36, 47
2. 33, 56, 65, 76
3. 17, 32, 46, 59
4. 19, 26, 39, 89
5. 319, 351, 721, 976
6. 572, 711, 897, 999
7. 100, 124, 231, 702
8. 308, 416, 596, 788
9. 36, 98, 102, 419
10. 42, 56, 789, 813

Page 7
1. 43, 15, 39, 61
2. 1, 45, 8, 42
3. 49, 38, 49, 9
4. 55, 36, 27, 65

Page 8
1. 112, 131, 210, 207
2. 148, 76, 542, 112
3. 105, 207, 945, 321
4. 205, 305, 550, 235

Page 9
1. 500 + 60 + 2
2. 900 + 50 + 3
3. 300 + 70 + 5
4. 600 + 10 + 7
5. 100 + 0 + 9
6. 7 hundreds + 4 tens + 9 ones
7. 5 hundreds + 1 ten + 4 ones
8. 9 hundreds + 3 tens + 6 ones
9. 3 hundreds + 9 tens + 8 ones
10. 6 hundreds + 1 ten + 7 ones

Page 10
1. ones
2. hundreds
3. thousands
4. thousands
5. tens
6. ones
7. 1
8. 4
9. 2
10. 7
11. 5
12. 7

Page 11

2	6	8			3	9	7
9			4	7	8	0	3
5		3	3	3	3		9
9	0	3	5		6	2	2
			4		5		
6	7	8		5	3	9	0
8	1	2	6		1	9	0
5		2	5	5	0		

Page 12
1. >, thousands
2. <, hundreds
3. >, ones
4. <, tens
5. <, tens
6. >, thousands
7. >, tens
8. 675; 6,075; 6,507; 6,705
9. 987; 4,279; 4,297; 7,942
10. 56; 506; 6,052; 6,502
Challenge: 9,631

Page 13
1. 5,863; 6,385; 5,813
2. 9,022; 9,004; 8,106
3. 6,683; 8,852; 7,932
4. 8,113; 7,621; 8,173

Page 14
1. 1,084; 1,084; 294
2. 1,465; 1,855; 2,301
3. 2,722; 3,929; 2,404
4. 3,826; 3,740; 2,207

Page 15
1.	2.	3.	4.
30	90	60	90
20	60	20	50
60	30	30	40
40	80	40	70
30	40	20	0
60	30	90	80

Page 16
1. 8, 10
2. 12, 18
3. 16, 14

Answer Key

Page 17

1.	4	2.	6	3.	2	4.	0
	6		9		1		0
	8		12		3		0
	10		15		4		0
	12		18		6		0
	14		21		5		0
	16		24		7		0
	18		27		8		0

Page 18

1.	8	2.	10	3.	20	4.	0
	12		15		9		20
	16		20		35		21
	20		25		5		32
	24		30		18		45
	28		35		14		10
	32		40		12		16
	36		45		18		28

Page 19

Page 20

1. 2 sets of two in 4 $4 \div 2 = 2$ 3 sets of two in 6 $6 \div 2 = 3$

2. 4 sets of two in 8 $8 \div 2 = 4$ 5 sets of two in 10 $10 \div 2 = 5$

3. 6 sets of two in 12 $12 \div 2 = 6$ 7 sets of two in 14 $14 \div 2 = 7$

Page 21

1. 2 sets of three in 6 $6 \div 3 = 2$ 3 sets of three in 9 $9 \div 3 = 3$

2. 4 sets of three in 12 $12 \div 3 = 4$ 5 sets of three in 15 $15 \div 3 = 5$

3. 6 sets of three in 18 $18 \div 3 = 6$ 7 sets of three in 21 $21 \div 3 = 7$

Page 22

1. 8, 2	2. 15, 3	3. 7, 2
4, 4	3, 3	14, 7

4. 8, 3	5. 6, 30	6. 28, 7
3, 8	5, 5	7, 28

7. $12 \div 4 = 3$ $18 \div 6 = 3$ $21 \div 3 = 7$
   $12 \div 3 = 4$ $18 \div 3 = 6$ $21 \div 7 = 3$

Page 23

3 Groups of 5

1.	2	2.	2	3.	2	4.	2
	3		3		5		3
	4		4		5		10
	5		5		4		4
	6		6		5		9
	7		7		2		2
	8		8		4		6
	9		9		7		7

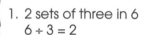

Page 24

1. 4, 0, 45, 32, 30
2. 7, 6, 3, 7, 8
3. 35, 16, 18, 5, 27
4. 3, 7, 2, 9, 4
   4 stamps

Page 25

1.	12	2.	14	3.	16	4.	18, 9
	18		21		24		27, 9
	24		28		32		36, 9
	30		35		40		45, 9
	36		42		48		54, 9
	42		49		56		63, 9
	48		56		64		72, 9
	54		63		72		81, 9

Page 26

1. 87, 72, 192, 52
2. 64, 165, 108, 36
3. 488, 364, 141, 819
4. 196, 272, 240, 98

Page 27

1. 954; 820; 2,448
2. 1,896; 256; 2,331
3. 700; 2,032; 858

Page 28

1. 108 feet
2. 2,800 pounds
3. 680 pounds

Page 29

1. 3 birds
2. 5 loaves
3. 5 bananas
4. 7 groups

Page 30

1. 3 pounds
2. 6 cards
3. 7 books
4. 7 babies

Sets in Multiplication

Write the numbers that name the set.

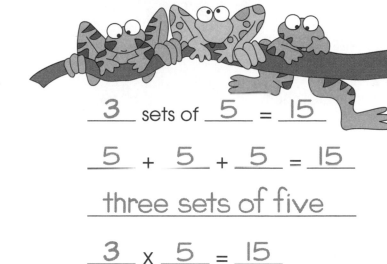

_3_ sets of _5_ = 15

_5_ + _5_ + _5_ = 15

three sets of five

_3_ x _5_ = 15

Try it!

1.

_____ sets of _____ = _____

_____ + _____ = _____

_____

_____ X _____ = _____

_____ sets of _____ = _____

_____ + _____ + _____ + _____ = _____

_____

_____ X _____ = _____

2.

_____ sets of _____ = _____

_____ + _____ + _____ = _____

_____

_____ X _____ = _____

_____ sets of _____ = _____

_____ + _____ + _____ + _____ = _____

_____

_____ X _____ = _____

Multiplication Sets

2 sets.
3 in each set.
2 x **3** = **6**

Rain forests

Write the problem that describes each set.

1.

 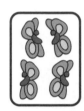 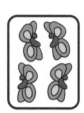

_____ X _____ = _____   _____ X _____ = _____

2.

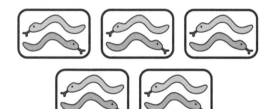     

_____ X _____ = _____   _____ X _____ = _____

3.

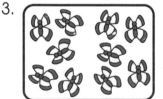 

_____ X _____ = _____   _____ X _____ = _____

Multiplication Equations Described as an Array

Add or Multiply

You are repeating addition when you multiply.

$3 \times 2 = 6$
$2 + 2 + 2 = 6$

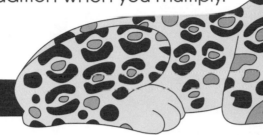
Ocelot

Write the addition and multiplication problems.

1. $4 \times 4 = 16$

___ + ___ + ___ + ___ = ___

$3 + 3 + 3 + 3 + 3 = 15$

___ X ___ = ___

2. $5 \times 9 = 45$

___ + ___ + ___ + ___ + ___ = ___

$6 + 6 + 6 + 6 + 6 + 6 = 36$

___ X ___ = ___

3. $3 \times 3 = 9$

___ + ___ + ___ = ___

$8 + 8 = 16$

___ X ___ = ___

4. $3 \times 7 = 21$

___ + ___ + ___ = ___

$7 + 7 + 7 + 7 = 28$

___ X ___ = ___

5. $5 \times 7 = 35$

___ + ___ + ___ + ___ + ___ = ___

$9 + 9 + 9 + 9 + 9 = 45$

___ X ___ = ___

Multiplication Facts: 2s and 3s

Count by **2**s.

1. **2 x 1** = _____

   2 x 2 = _____

   2 x 3 = _____

   2 x 4 = _____

   2 x 5 = _____

   2 x 6 = _____

   2 x 7 = _____

   2 x 8 = _____

   2 x 9 = _____

   2 x 10 = _____

Count by **3**s.

2. **3 x 1** = _____

   3 x 2 = _____

   3 x 3 = _____

   3 x 4 = _____

   3 x 5 = _____

   3 x 6 = _____

   3 x 7 = _____

   3 x 8 = _____

   3 x 9 = _____

   3 x 10 = _____

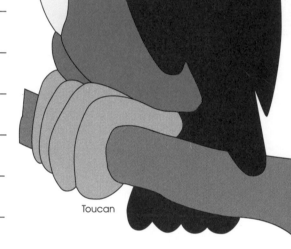

Toucan

You get the same answer in multiplication, even if the order of the factors is changed.

2 sets of **5** and **5** sets of **2** are the same.
2 x 5 = 5 x 2. **2 x 5 = 10**. **5 x 2 = 10**.

3. **2 x 4** = _____

   3 x 6 = _____

   3 x 4 = _____

   7 x 2 = _____

   2 x 3 = _____

4 x 2 = _____

6 x 3 = _____

4 x 3 = _____

2 x 7 = _____

3 x 2 = _____

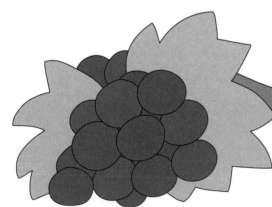

Practice these facts so you can say the answers fast!

Multiplication Facts: 4s and 5s

Long-tongued fruit bats

Count by **4**s.

1. 4 x 1 = _____
   4 x 2 = _____
   4 x 3 = _____
   4 x 4 = _____
   4 x 5 = _____
   4 x 6 = _____
   4 x 7 = _____
   4 x 8 = _____
   4 x 9 = _____
   4 x 10 = _____

Count by **5**s.

2. 5 x 1 = _____
   5 x 2 = _____
   5 x 3 = _____
   5 x 4 = _____
   5 x 5 = _____
   5 x 6 = _____
   5 x 7 = _____
   5 x 8 = _____
   5 x 9 = _____
   5 x 10 = _____

Draw sets for the problems below.

3. 4 x 3 = 12   4 x 4 = 16   5 x 4 = 20

4. 5 x 6 = 30   5 x 1 = 5   5 x 3 = 15

Multiplication Facts: 6s and 7s

Count by **6**s.

1. **6** x **1** = _____
    6 x **2** = _____
    6 x **3** = _____
    6 x **4** = _____
    6 x **5** = _____
    6 x **6** = _____
    6 x **7** = _____
    6 x **8** = _____
    6 x **9** = _____
    6 x **10** = _____

Count by **7**s.

2. **7** x **1** = _____
    7 x **2** = _____
    7 x **3** = _____
    7 x **4** = _____
    7 x **5** = _____
    7 x **6** = _____
    7 x **7** = _____
    7 x **8** = _____
    7 x **9** = _____
    7 x **10** = _____

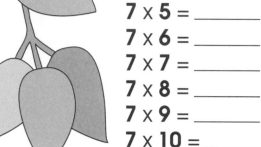

Red howler monkeys

Write the multiplication problems and answers for the following sets.

3. **6** sets of **4** _____

4. **2** sets of **7** _____

5. **6** sets of **7** _____

6. **5** sets of **6** _____

7. **8** sets of **7** _____

8. **7** sets of **3** _____

9. **6** sets of **8** _____

10. **4** sets of **7** _____

Multiplication Facts: 8s and 9s

Here's a trick when you count by **9**s. The numbers in the answer total **9** when you add them together.

$$9 \times 3 = 27$$

$$2 + 7 = 9$$

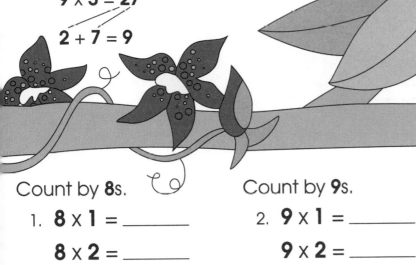
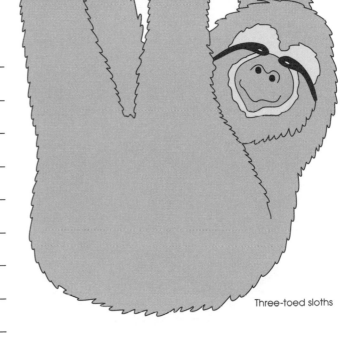

Count by **8**s.

1. $8 \times 1 =$ _____

   $8 \times 2 =$ _____

   $8 \times 3 =$ _____

   $8 \times 4 =$ _____

   $8 \times 5 =$ _____

   $8 \times 6 =$ _____

   $8 \times 7 =$ _____

   $8 \times 8 =$ _____

   $8 \times 9 =$ _____

   $8 \times 10 =$ _____

Count by **9**s.

2. $9 \times 1 =$ _____

   $9 \times 2 =$ _____

   $9 \times 3 =$ _____

   $9 \times 4 =$ _____

   $9 \times 5 =$ _____

   $9 \times 6 =$ _____

   $9 \times 7 =$ _____

   $9 \times 8 =$ _____

   $9 \times 9 =$ _____

   $9 \times 10 =$ _____

Three-toed sloths

Here is a mini-review.

3.
$$\begin{array}{r} 4 \\ \times\,4 \\ \hline \end{array}$$
$$\begin{array}{r} 7 \\ \times\,3 \\ \hline \end{array}$$
$$\begin{array}{r} 8 \\ \times\,4 \\ \hline \end{array}$$
$$\begin{array}{r} 5 \\ \times\,9 \\ \hline \end{array}$$

4.
$$\begin{array}{r} 4 \\ \times\,7 \\ \hline \end{array}$$
$$\begin{array}{r} 3 \\ \times\,5 \\ \hline \end{array}$$
$$\begin{array}{r} 6 \\ \times\,4 \\ \hline \end{array}$$
$$\begin{array}{r} 9 \\ \times\,6 \\ \hline \end{array}$$

Multiplication Facts: 0s and 10s

When multiplying by **0**, the answer is always zero because there is nothing in the sets.

5 sets of **0** is $0 + 0 + 0 + 0 + 0$.
It is also **5 x 0**.
$5 \times 0 = 0$.

Count by **0**s.

1. $0 \times 1 =$ _____
   $0 \times 2 =$ _____
   $0 \times 3 =$ _____
   $0 \times 4 =$ _____
   $0 \times 5 =$ _____
   $0 \times 6 =$ _____
   $0 \times 7 =$ _____
   $0 \times 8 =$ _____
   $0 \times 9 =$ _____
   $0 \times 10 =$ _____

Count by **10**s.

2. $10 \times 1 =$ _____
   $10 \times 2 =$ _____
   $10 \times 3 =$ _____
   $10 \times 4 =$ _____
   $10 \times 5 =$ _____
   $10 \times 6 =$ _____
   $10 \times 7 =$ _____
   $10 \times 8 =$ _____
   $10 \times 9 =$ _____
   $10 \times 10 =$ _____

Giant anteater

Did you notice a pattern in the answers? The answer is always the same number you multiplied by **10** with a **0** after it.

Leaf-cutting ants

If there are **10** tens in **100**, how many tens are in **200**? _____

Name the Missing Factors

$5 \times 7 = 35$ **5** and **7** are called **factors**.
35 Is called the **product**.

Find the factors.

1. $5 \times \underline{\hspace{1cm}} = 20$ $9 \times \underline{\hspace{1cm}} = 63$

2. $9 \times \underline{\hspace{1cm}} = 9$ $10 \times \underline{\hspace{1cm}} = 40$

3. $\underline{\hspace{1cm}} \times 8 = 32$ $\underline{\hspace{1cm}} \times 4 = 24$

4. $9 \times \underline{\hspace{1cm}} = 81$ $6 \times \underline{\hspace{1cm}} = 42$

5. $\underline{\hspace{1cm}} \times 7 = 14$ $\underline{\hspace{1cm}} \times 7 = 49$

6. $\underline{\hspace{1cm}} \times 10 = 90$ $\underline{\hspace{1cm}} \times 10 = 50$

7. $3 \times \underline{\hspace{1cm}} = 24$ $9 \times \underline{\hspace{1cm}} = 72$

8. $4 \times \underline{\hspace{1cm}} = 12$ $8 \times \underline{\hspace{1cm}} = 64$

White-lipped
peccaries

One-Digit Multiplication

Multiplication problems can be written **2** ways.

$$\begin{array}{r} 4 \\ \times\,3 \\ \hline 12 \end{array}$$ is the same as **3 × 4 = 12**

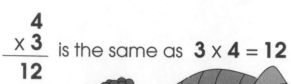

Multiply the following problems.

1. **3 × 2 =**

2. **3 × 9 =**

3. **4 × 5 =**

4. **4 × 9 =**

5. **5 × 6 =**

6. **5 × 9 =**

7. **6 × 2 =**

8. **6 × 7 =**

9. **7 × 4 =**

10. **7 × 8 =**

Ruby-topaz
hummingbird

Praying mantis

11. $$\begin{array}{r} \mathbf{9} \\ \times\,\mathbf{4} \\ \hline \end{array}$$ $$\begin{array}{r} \mathbf{9} \\ \times\,\mathbf{9} \\ \hline \end{array}$$

12. $$\begin{array}{r} \mathbf{10} \\ \times\,\ \mathbf{5} \\ \hline \end{array}$$ $$\begin{array}{r} \mathbf{10} \\ \times\,\ \mathbf{8} \\ \hline \end{array}$$

13. $$\begin{array}{r} \mathbf{5} \\ \times\,\mathbf{3} \\ \hline \end{array}$$ $$\begin{array}{r} \mathbf{5} \\ \times\,\mathbf{4} \\ \hline \end{array}$$

14. $$\begin{array}{r} \mathbf{8} \\ \times\,\mathbf{4} \\ \hline \end{array}$$ $$\begin{array}{r} \mathbf{6} \\ \times\,\mathbf{6} \\ \hline \end{array}$$

Find the Product

The first player to get four in a row wins!

How to play:

1. You'll need two or more players.
2. Take turns calling out facts such as **7 x 5**.
3. Using a marker of a different color for each player, place your answer where the two numbers meet on the chart.
   Example: **7 x 5 = 35**
4. Try to block your opponent from getting four in a row.

Use this chart to check multiplication problems on other pages.

	0	1	2	3	4	5	6	7	8	9
0										
1										
2										
3										
4										
5										
6										
7										
8										
9										

Multiplication Facts Review

How many minutes will it take you to go from the waterfall to the village? Call out the answers to a friend. Time yourself. Can you do it in less than three minutes? Practice until you can do the whole thing in less than one minute!

$6 \times 7 =$

$3 \times 4 =$

$8 \times 8 =$

$2 \times 7 =$

$7 \times 3 =$

$0 \times 7 =$

$9 \times 9 =$

$9 \times 10 =$

$8 \times 2 =$

$4 \times 6 =$

$5 \times 8 =$

$5 \times 5 =$

$4 \times 4 =$

$7 \times 6 =$

$2 \times 9 =$

$6 \times 5 =$

$1 \times 0 =$

$10 \times 3 =$

$9 \times 4 =$

$6 \times 10 =$

$10 \times 10 =$

$8 \times 7 =$

$3 \times 3 =$

Multiplying 2 Numbers by 1 Number

If you know your facts, you can multiply any two numbers together.

First, multiply the ones: **3 x 3 = 9**. Write the answer in the ones column.

$$\begin{array}{r} \text{tens} \ \text{ones} \\ 23 \\ \times\ 3 \\ \hline 9 \end{array}$$

Second, multiply the tens: **3 x 2 = 6**. Write the answer in the tens column.

$$\begin{array}{r} \text{tens} \ \text{ones} \\ 23 \\ \times\ 3 \\ \hline 69 \end{array}$$

3 x 23 = 69.
This can also be written **23 x 3 = 69**.

Multiply the following problems.

1.
$$\begin{array}{r} 14 \\ \times\ 2 \\ \hline \end{array} \qquad \begin{array}{r} 12 \\ \times\ 4 \\ \hline \end{array} \qquad \begin{array}{r} 23 \\ \times\ 2 \\ \hline \end{array}$$

2.
$$\begin{array}{r} 33 \\ \times\ 3 \\ \hline \end{array} \qquad \begin{array}{r} 24 \\ \times\ 2 \\ \hline \end{array} \qquad \begin{array}{r} 11 \\ \times\ 7 \\ \hline \end{array}$$

3.
$$\begin{array}{r} 32 \\ \times\ 3 \\ \hline \end{array} \qquad \begin{array}{r} 10 \\ \times\ 4 \\ \hline \end{array} \qquad \begin{array}{r} 13 \\ \times\ 2 \\ \hline \end{array}$$

Up to **3** plant and animal species are becoming extinct each day. How many could be extinct in **12** days? _____

Multiplication with Regrouping

Sometimes you need to regroup when you multiply.

```
  3
 45
x 7
----
  5
```

First, multiply the ones: **7 x 5 = 35**.
Regroup the **35** into **3** tens and **5** ones.
Write down the **5** ones and put the **3**
tens above the tens column.

```
  3
 45
x 7
----
315
```

Second, multiply the tens: **7 x 4 = 28**.
Add the extra **3** tens to the answer.
28 + 3 = 31.

Now you try it!

Giant armadillo

1.
```
  42        98        74        34        78        64
x  6      x  2      x  4      x  3      x  2      x  5
```

2.
```
  63        18        55        19        28        45
x  9      x  3      x  5      x  9      x  3      x  5
```

Try these.

3. **4 x 2 x 3 =** _____   **5 x 2 x 8 =** _____   **6 x 2 x 3 =** _____

Multiplying 3 Numbers by 1 Number

$$\begin{array}{r} {}^{3\ 1}\!452 \\ \times \quad 6 \\ \hline 12 \end{array}$$

Multiply the ones. Regroup.
Multiply the tens. Add the extra tens.
5 x 6 = 30 + 1 = 31 tens.
Regroup.

$$\begin{array}{r} {}^{3\ 1}\!452 \\ \times \quad 6 \\ \hline 2,712 \end{array}$$

Multiply the hundreds. **6 x 4 = 24**.
Add the extra hundreds.
24 + 3 = 27.
Write the answer.

It takes a little longer, but you can do it!
Find your answers in the puzzle below.

1.
$$\begin{array}{r} 126 \\ \times \quad 4 \end{array}$$
$$\begin{array}{r} 472 \\ \times \quad 2 \end{array}$$
$$\begin{array}{r} 975 \\ \times \quad 4 \end{array}$$

2.
$$\begin{array}{r} 134 \\ \times \quad 7 \end{array}$$
$$\begin{array}{r} 813 \\ \times \quad 3 \end{array}$$
$$\begin{array}{r} 144 \\ \times \quad 8 \end{array}$$

3.
$$\begin{array}{r} 135 \\ \times \quad 2 \end{array}$$
$$\begin{array}{r} 292 \\ \times \quad 5 \end{array}$$
$$\begin{array}{r} 224 \\ \times \quad 9 \end{array}$$

2	1	1	5	2	9
5	0	4	4	7	4
3	3	1	9	0	4
9	0	8	6	4	2
0	2	4	3	9	7
0	1	4	9	3	8

Sulphur-crested
cockatoo

Multiplying 4 Numbers by 1 Number

$$\begin{array}{r}
{\scriptstyle 2\ \ 11}\\
5{,}432\\
\times\qquad 6\\
\hline
32{,}592
\end{array}$$

Multiply the ones. Regroup.
Multiply the tens. Regroup.
Multiply the hundreds. Regroup.
Multiply the thousands. **6 x 5 = 30 + 2 = 32.**

Try a few problems!

1.
$$\begin{array}{r} 2{,}222 \\ \times\ \ \ 3 \\ \hline \end{array}\qquad\begin{array}{r} 3{,}141 \\ \times\ \ \ 5 \\ \hline \end{array}\qquad\begin{array}{r} 1{,}338 \\ \times\ \ \ 6 \\ \hline \end{array}$$

2.
$$\begin{array}{r} 9{,}214 \\ \times\ \ \ 4 \\ \hline \end{array}\qquad\begin{array}{r} 7{,}768 \\ \times\ \ \ 2 \\ \hline \end{array}\qquad\begin{array}{r} 5{,}261 \\ \times\ \ \ 3 \\ \hline \end{array}$$

3.
$$\begin{array}{r} 3{,}105 \\ \times\ \ \ 7 \\ \hline \end{array}\qquad\begin{array}{r} 2{,}025 \\ \times\ \ \ 8 \\ \hline \end{array}\qquad\begin{array}{r} 6{,}350 \\ \times\ \ \ 5 \\ \hline \end{array}$$

4. Brazil nuts come from the fruit of a tree found near the Amazon River. Each fruit can have up to **24** nuts. How many nuts can **8** fruits have? _____

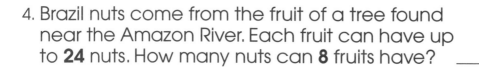

Multiplying with Zeros

When you multiply by zeros, count the zeros.
Write them down. Then multiply what's left.

$$\begin{array}{r} 80 \\ \times\ 40 \\ \hline 3{,}200 \end{array}$$

There are **2** zeros. **8 x 4 = 32**.
The answer is **32** with the **2** zeros.

Brazilian tapir

Multiply the following problems.
Can you do these in your head?

1.
$$\begin{array}{r} 20 \\ \times\ 30 \\ \hline \end{array} \qquad \begin{array}{r} 80 \\ \times\ 70 \\ \hline \end{array} \qquad \begin{array}{r} 60 \\ \times\ 50 \\ \hline \end{array} \qquad \begin{array}{r} 200 \\ \times\quad 8 \\ \hline \end{array} \qquad \begin{array}{r} 600 \\ \times\ 600 \\ \hline \end{array}$$

2.
$$\begin{array}{r} 70 \\ \times\ 6 \\ \hline \end{array} \qquad \begin{array}{r} 50 \\ \times\ 8 \\ \hline \end{array} \qquad \begin{array}{r} 90 \\ \times\ 4 \\ \hline \end{array} \qquad \begin{array}{r} 300 \\ \times\ 40 \\ \hline \end{array} \qquad \begin{array}{r} 200 \\ \times\ 300 \\ \hline \end{array}$$

3. Some rain forest trees produce **650,000** flowers
   in a single day. How many can be produced
   in **3** days?   _____

4. Close to **45** kinds of orchids have been found
   blooming in a single rain forest tree. If **10** trees
   had the same number of different kinds, how
   many kinds of orchids would you find?   _____

Multiplying 2 Numbers by 2 Numbers

$$\begin{array}{r} \overset{3}{54} \\ \times\,38 \\ \hline 432 \end{array}$$

Multiply the ones. **8 x 4 = 32**. Regroup.
Multiply the tens. **8 x 5 = 40 + 3 = 43**.

$$\begin{array}{r} \overset{1}{54} \\ \times\,38 \\ \hline 432 \\ 1620 \\ \hline 2,052 \end{array}$$

Because the **3** is in the tens place, the answer begins in the tens place.
Hold the ones place by adding a zero.
Multiply the ones. **3 x 4 = 12**. Regroup.
Multiply the tens. **3 x 5 = 15 + 1 = 16**.
Add **432 + 1620** together for the final answer.

Arrau River turtle

Multiply the two factors to find the products.

1.
$$\begin{array}{r} 31 \\ \times\,77 \end{array} \qquad \begin{array}{r} 46 \\ \times\,22 \end{array} \qquad \begin{array}{r} 93 \\ \times\,11 \end{array}$$

2.
$$\begin{array}{r} 84 \\ \times\,17 \end{array} \qquad \begin{array}{r} 53 \\ \times\,44 \end{array} \qquad \begin{array}{r} 62 \\ \times\,25 \end{array}$$

3. The Arrau River turtle is one of the largest freshwater turtles. It can lay up to **150** eggs in one year. How many eggs could it lay in **16** years? _____

4. Joshua has **23** classmates. He promised to send each of them a postcard from all **12** cities he plans to visit. How many postcards will he send?

_____

Branching Out with Multiplication

On the leaves of each branch, write two factors that equal the center product. The first one is done for you.

Learning About Division

There are three sets of **2** in **6**.

We can write a division problem
6 ÷ 3 = 2.
6 in all, divided by **3** sets = **2** in each set
or **6 ÷ 2 = 3**.
6 in all, divided by **2** in each set = **3** sets.

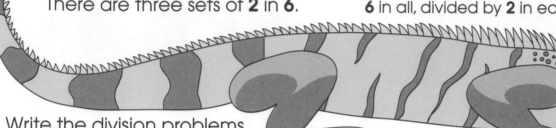

Write the division problems.

1.

Common iguana

_____ ÷ _____ = _____   _____ ÷ _____ = _____

_____ ÷ _____ = _____   _____ ÷ _____ = _____

2.

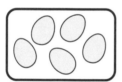 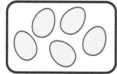     

_____ ÷ _____ = _____   _____ ÷ _____ = _____

_____ ÷ _____ = _____   _____ ÷ _____ = _____

3.

_____ ÷ _____ = _____   _____ ÷ _____ = _____

_____ ÷ _____ = _____   _____ ÷ _____ = _____

Division Facts

Multiplication Helps Division

If you know your multiplication facts, you are ready for division.

Here is a multiplication problem **4 x 3 = 12**

rewritten as a division problem: **12 ÷ 3 = 4**

or
12 ÷ 4 = 3.

 Okapi

Write the division problems for each multiplication problem.

1.   **8 x 7 = 56**   **4 x 9 = 36**   **5 x 5 = 25**

   _____ ÷ _____ = _____   _____ ÷ _____ = _____   _____ ÷ _____ = _____

   _____ ÷ _____ = _____   _____ ÷ _____ = _____

2.   **6 x 7 = 42**   **3 x 8 = 24**   **2 x 7 = 14**

   _____ ÷ _____ = _____   _____ ÷ _____ = _____   _____ ÷ _____ = _____

   _____ ÷ _____ = _____   _____ ÷ _____ = _____   _____ ÷ _____ = _____

3.   **7 x 5 = 35**   **8 x 9 = 72**   **4 x 8 = 32**

   _____ ÷ _____ = _____   _____ ÷ _____ = _____   _____ ÷ _____ = _____

   _____ ÷ _____ = _____   _____ ÷ _____ = _____   _____ ÷ _____ = _____

4. Joshua has **24** Brazil nuts to divide among
   6 friends. How many nuts will each friend get?   _____

5. Joshua has collected **63** stamps from different countries.
   He wants to divide them into **7** albums. How many stamps
   will go into each album?   _____

53

More Division Facts

$12 \div 3 = 4$ can also be written like this
This way is called **long division**.

$$3 \overline{)12}^{\,4}$$

There are three parts to a division problem.

horizontally

$$\underset{\text{dividend}}{12} \div \underset{\text{divisor}}{3} = \underset{\text{quotient}}{4}$$

long division

$$\underset{\text{divisor}}{3} \overline{)\underset{\text{dividend}}{12}}^{\;4\;\text{— quotient}}$$

Boa constrictor

Complete these problems by finding a divisor and a quotient.

1. $18 \div \underline{\hspace{1cm}} = \underline{\hspace{1cm}}$ $81 \div \underline{\hspace{1cm}} = \underline{\hspace{1cm}}$

   $30 \div \underline{\hspace{1cm}} = \underline{\hspace{1cm}}$ $63 \div \underline{\hspace{1cm}} = \underline{\hspace{1cm}}$

   $50 \div \underline{\hspace{1cm}} = \underline{\hspace{1cm}}$ $45 \div \underline{\hspace{1cm}} = \underline{\hspace{1cm}}$

Find the quotient for the following problems.

2. $72 \div 9 = \underline{\hspace{1cm}}$ $20 \div 5 = \underline{\hspace{1cm}}$

   $36 \div 6 = \underline{\hspace{1cm}}$ $36 \div 9 = \underline{\hspace{1cm}}$

   $25 \div 5 = \underline{\hspace{1cm}}$ $60 \div 10 = \underline{\hspace{1cm}}$

Write the multiplication problem that goes with each division problem.

3. $16 \div 4 = 4$ $\underline{\hspace{5cm}}$

   $27 \div 3 = 9$ $\underline{\hspace{5cm}}$

   $20 \div 5 = 4$ $\underline{\hspace{5cm}}$

Division Facts

Another Way of Writing Division Problems

Giant otter

Rewrite these problems using long division.

1. $81 \div 9 = 9$ $\boxed{}$ $8 \div 2 = 4$ $\boxed{}$

2. $56 \div 8 = 7$ $\boxed{}$ $14 \div 7 = 2$ $\boxed{}$

Find the quotient by thinking of the multiplication fact that goes with each division problem. Line up your answer with the tens and ones in the dividend.

3.
$3\overline{)24}$ $6\overline{)42}$

$7\overline{)49}$ $2\overline{)20}$

$9\overline{)90}$ $5\overline{)35}$

$4\overline{)4}$ $8\overline{)64}$

Beginning Long Division

Dividing 2 Numbers by 1 Number

There are five steps of dividing to remember.
1. Divide.
2. Multiply.
3. Subtract.
4. Compare.
5. Bring down the next number.

 1. Divide

$$\begin{array}{r} 3 \\ 3\overline{)96} \end{array}$$

Divide the tens.
$9 \div 3 = 3$

2. Multiply

$$\begin{array}{r} 3 \\ 3\overline{)96} \\ \underline{9} \end{array}$$

$3 \times 3 = 9$
Write the **9**
under the **9**.

3. Subtract

$$\begin{array}{r} 3 \\ 3\overline{)96} \\ -\underline{9} \\ 0 \end{array}$$

4. Compare to make sure the divisor is smaller than the dividend.

5. Bring down the next number.

$$\begin{array}{r} 3 \\ 3\overline{)96} \\ -\underline{9} \\ 06 \end{array}$$

Repeat the first five steps to complete the problem.

Divide

$$\begin{array}{r} 32 \\ 3\overline{)96} \\ -\underline{9} \\ 06 \end{array}$$

$6 \div 3 = 2$

Multiply

$$\begin{array}{r} 32 \\ 3\overline{)96} \\ -\underline{9} \\ 06 \\ 6 \end{array}$$

$3 \times 2 = 6$
Write the **6** under the **6**.

Subtract

$$\begin{array}{r} 32 \\ 3\overline{)96} \\ -\underline{9} \\ 06 \\ -\underline{6} \\ 0 \end{array}$$

There is no other number to bring down, so the problem is finished.

Check
To check your answer, multiply the quotient (answer) by the divisor.

$$\begin{array}{r} 32 \\ \times\ \ 3 \\ \hline 96 \end{array}$$

Ruffed lemur

Try these!

1.

$8\overline{)96}$ Check $\times$ _____

$4\overline{)92}$ Check $\times$ _____

$2\overline{)84}$ Check $\times$ _____

Dividing 3 Numbers by 1 Number

```
    120
5 | 600
  - 5
    10
  - 10
    00
  -  0
     0
```

Follow the same five steps.
1. Divide.
2. Multiply.
3. Subtract.
4. Compare.
5. Bring down.

Jaguar

Check
```
  120
x   5
  600
```

To check your answer, multiply the quotient (answer) by the divisor.

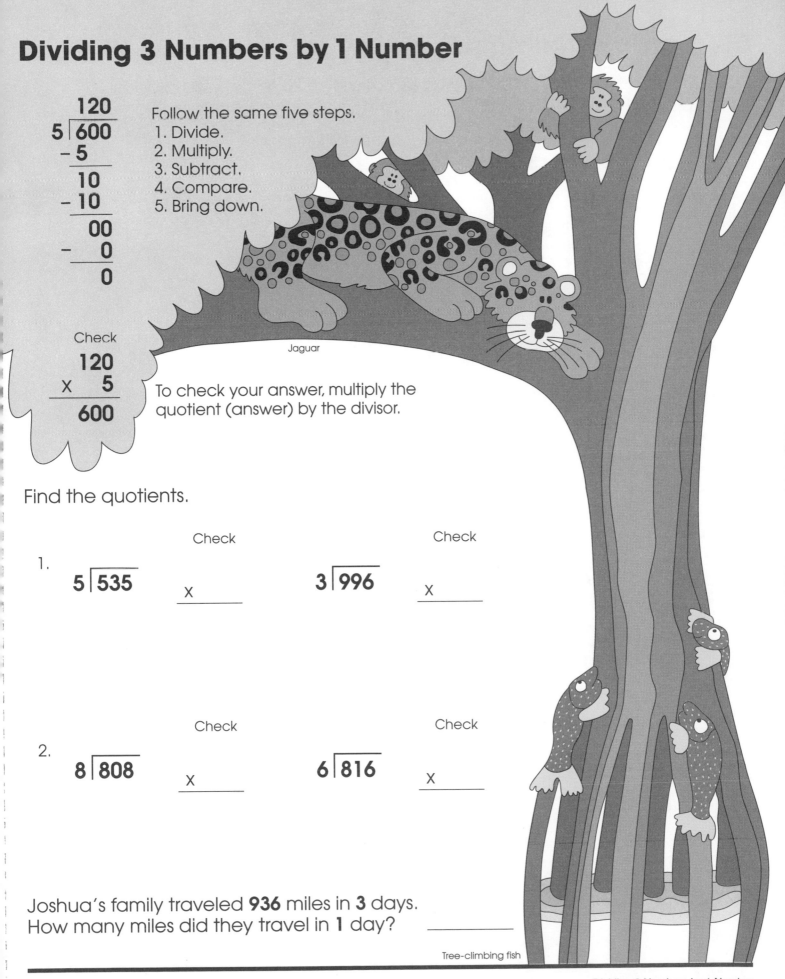

Find the quotients.

1.

               Check   Check

5 | 535   x _____   3 | 996   x _____

2.

               Check   Check

8 | 808   x _____   6 | 816   x _____

Tree-climbing fish

Joshua's family traveled **936** miles in **3** days.
How many miles did they travel in **1** day? _____

Division with Remainders

Sometimes a division problem has a **remainder**. If **23** frogs were divided into groups of **3**, there would be **7** groups of **3**, with **2** frogs remaining.

7 R2 The **R** stands for **Remainder**.

$$23 \div 3 = 7 \text{ R2} \quad \text{or} \quad 3\overline{)23}$$

$$\begin{array}{r} 7 \\ \times\,3 \\ \hline 21 \\ +\,2 \\ \hline 23 \end{array}$$

$$\begin{array}{r} 3\overline{)23} \\ -21 \\ \hline 2 \end{array}$$

Check:
To check, multiply the quotient by the divisor. Then add the remainder.

Tree frog

Solve these problems.

1.
$4\overline{)47}$

Check

x _____

+ _____

$6\overline{)56}$

Check

x _____

+ _____

$5\overline{)209}$

Check

x _____

+ _____

2.
$2\overline{)95}$

Check

x _____

+ _____

$7\overline{)89}$

Check

x _____

+ _____

$6\overline{)829}$

Check

x _____

+ _____

3.
$4\overline{)399}$

Check

x _____

+ _____

$3\overline{)617}$

Check

x _____

+ _____

$5\overline{)512}$

Check

x _____

+ _____

Amazing Facts!

Solve the problems to find the answers.

Many foods that we eat today were originally found in the rain forests.

Foods such as _____ , sugarcane, oranges, and _____ come from rain forest trees and plants.

Indigo macaw

O

1. **350 ÷ 7 =** _____

R

120 ÷ 4 = _____

C

100 ÷ 4 = _____

N

2. **63 ÷ 7 =** _____

L

300 ÷ 4 = _____

E

144 ÷ 12 = _____

O

3. **250 ÷ 5 =** _____

T

90 ÷ 2 = _____

L

808 ÷ 8 = _____

D

4. **162 ÷ 9 =** _____

A

144 ÷ 2 = _____

C

250 ÷ 10 = _____

H

5. **180 ÷ 3 =** _____

C

150 ÷ 6 = _____

O

450 ÷ 9 = _____

____ ____ ____ ____ , ____ ____ ____ ____ ____ ____ ____ ____ ____

25   50   30   9   25   60   50   25   50   101   72   45   12

Division Review

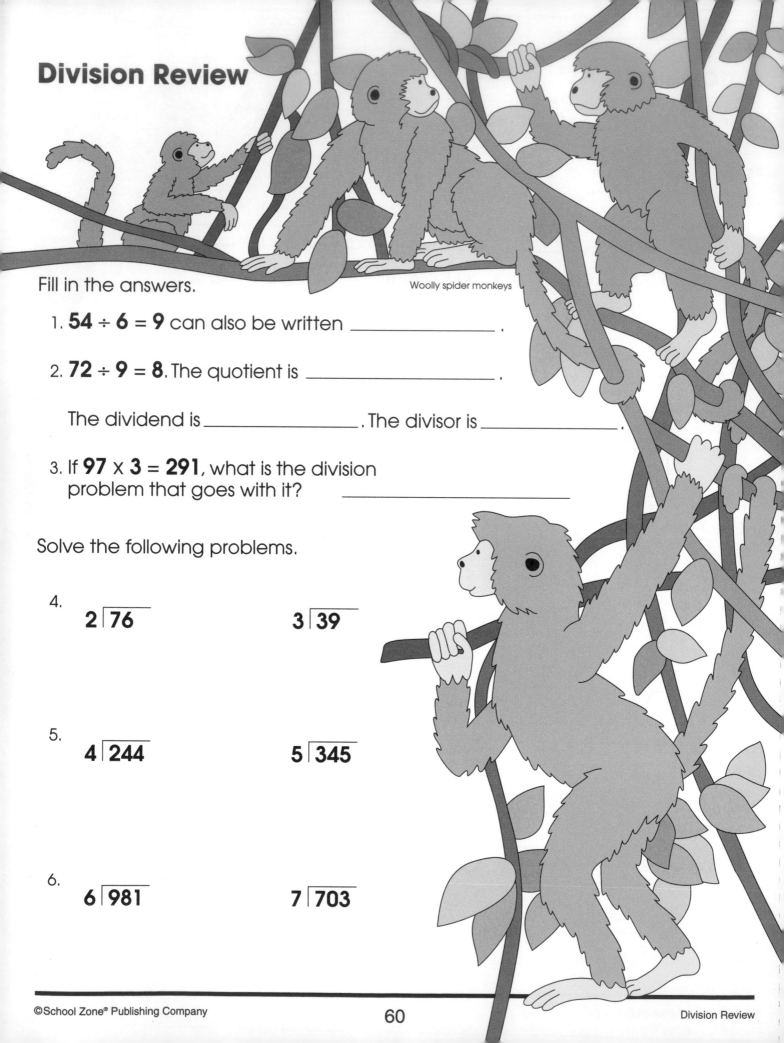

Woolly spider monkeys

Fill in the answers.

1. **54 ÷ 6 = 9** can also be written _____ .

2. **72 ÷ 9 = 8**. The quotient is _____ .

   The dividend is _____ . The divisor is _____ .

3. If **97 x 3 = 291**, what is the division
   problem that goes with it? _____

Solve the following problems.

4.
   $2\overline{)76}$ $3\overline{)39}$

5.
   $4\overline{)244}$ $5\overline{)345}$

6.
   $6\overline{)981}$ $7\overline{)703}$

Division Review

Multiplication or Division?

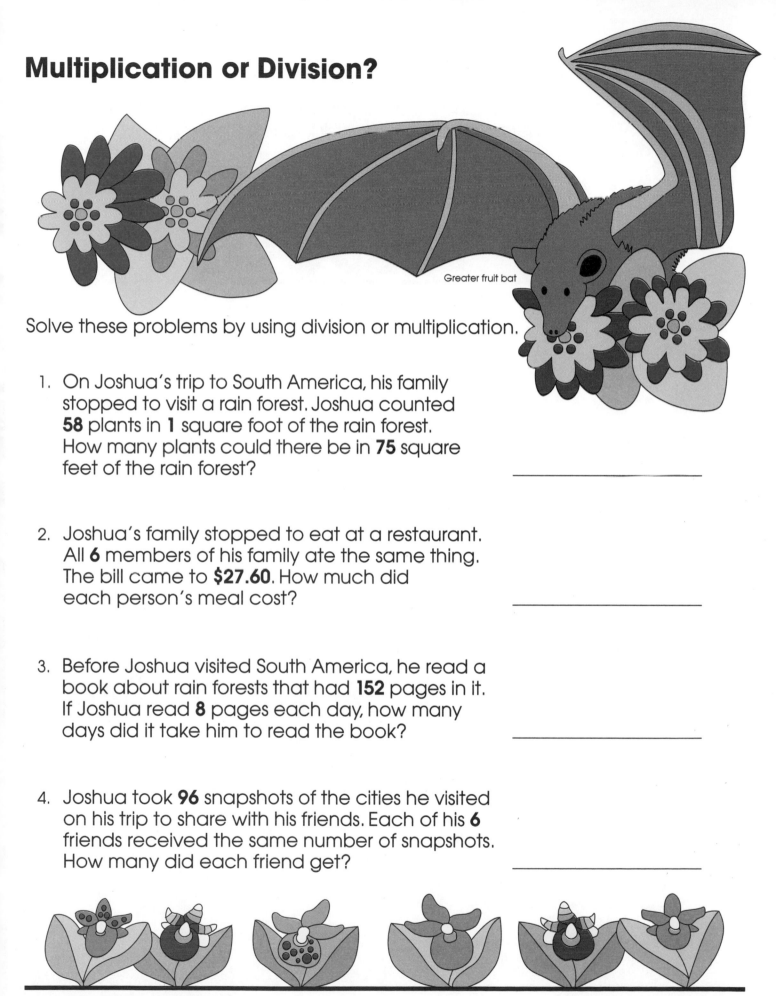

Greater fruit bat

Solve these problems by using division or multiplication.

1. On Joshua's trip to South America, his family
   stopped to visit a rain forest. Joshua counted
   58 plants in **1** square foot of the rain forest.
   How many plants could there be in **75** square
   feet of the rain forest?

   _____

2. Joshua's family stopped to eat at a restaurant.
   All **6** members of his family ate the same thing.
   The bill came to **$27.60**. How much did
   each person's meal cost?

   _____

3. Before Joshua visited South America, he read a
   book about rain forests that had **152** pages in it.
   If Joshua read **8** pages each day, how many
   days did it take him to read the book?

   _____

4. Joshua took **96** snapshots of the cities he visited
   on his trip to share with his friends. Each of his **6**
   friends received the same number of snapshots.
   How many did each friend get?

   _____

Combining Multiplication and Division

Here's a fun activity for you using both multiplication and division. Use the first four numbers in order by multiplying or dividing to make the fifth number. You may want to use a calculator.

9 9 4 2 8

$9 \div 9 = 1 \times 4 = 4 \times 2 = 8$

Red piranhas

Your turn!

1. **6** 5 3 2 5 _____

2. **10** 5 4 2 4 _____

3. **49** 7 6 6 7 _____

4. **90** 10 3 6 18 _____

Manatees

Answer Key

Page 33

1. 2 sets of 2 = 4
   2 + 2 = 4
   two sets of two
   2 x 2 = 4

   4 sets of 2 = 8
   2 + 2 + 2 + 2 = 8
   four sets of two
   4 x 2 = 8

2. 3 sets of 3 = 9
   3 + 3 + 3 = 9
   three sets of three
   3 x 3 = 9

   4 sets of 4 = 16
   4 + 4 + 4 + 4 = 16
   four sets of four
   4 x 4 = 16

Page 34

1. 3 x 4 = 12   4 x 5 = 20
2. 5 x 2 = 10   3 x 9 = 27
3. 2 x 10 = 20   4 x 9 = 36

Page 35

1. 4 + 4 + 4 + 4 = 16   5 x 3 = 15
2. 9 + 9 + 9 + 9 + 9 = 45   6 x 6 = 36
3. 3 + 3 + 3 = 9   2 x 8 = 16
4. 7 + 7 + 7 = 21   4 x 7 = 28
5. 7 + 7 + 7 + 7 + 7 = 35   5 x 9 = 45

Page 36

1.	2	2.	3
	4		6
	6		9
	8		12
	10		15
	12		18
	14		21
	16		24
	18		27
	20		30

3. 8, 8
   18, 18
   12, 12
   14, 14
   6, 6

Page 37

1.	4	2.	5
	8		10
	12		15
	16		20
	20		25
	24		30
	28		35
	32		40
	36		45
	40		50

3.

4.

Page 38

1.	6	2.	7
	12		14
	18		21
	24		28
	30		35
	36		42
	42		49
	48		56
	54		63
	60		70

3. 6 x 4 = 24
4. 2 x 7 = 14
5. 6 x 7 = 42
6. 5 x 6 = 30
7. 8 x 7 = 56
8. 7 x 3 = 21
9. 6 x 8 = 48
10. 4 x 7 = 28

Page 39

1.	8	2.	9
	16		18
	24		27
	32		36
	40		45
	48		54
	56		63
	64		72
	72		81
	80		90

3. 16, 21, 32, 45
4. 28, 15, 24, 54

Page 40

1.	0	2.	10
	0		20
	0		30
	0		40
	0		50
	0		60
	0		70
	0		80
	0		90
	0		100

20 tens in 200

Page 41

1. 5 x 4 = 20   9 x 7 = 63
2. 9 x 1 = 9   10 x 4 = 40
3. 4 x 8 = 32   6 x 4 = 24
4. 9 x 9 = 81   6 x 7 = 42
5. 2 x 7 = 14   7 x 7 = 49
6. 9 x 10 = 90   5 x 10 = 50
7. 3 x 8 = 24   9 x 8 = 72
8. 4 x 3 = 12   8 x 8 = 64

Page 42

1. 6   11. 36, 81
2. 27   12. 50, 80
3. 20   13. 15, 20
4. 36   14. 32, 36
5. 30
6. 45
7. 12
8. 42
9. 28
10. 56

Page 43

	0	1	2	3	4	5	6	7	8	9
0	0	0	0	0	0	0	0	0	0	0
1	0	1	2	3	4	5	6	7	8	9
2	0	2	4	6	8	10	12	14	16	18
3	0	3	6	9	12	15	18	21	24	27
4	0	4	8	12	16	20	24	28	32	36
5	0	5	10	15	20	25	30	35	40	45
6	0	6	12	18	24	30	36	42	48	54
7	0	7	14	21	28	35	42	49	56	63
8	0	8	16	24	32	40	48	56	64	72
9	0	9	18	27	36	45	54	63	72	81

Page 47

1. 504; 944; 3,900
2. 938; 2,439; 1,152
3. 270; 1,460; 2,016

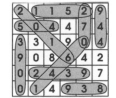

Page 44

42, 12, 64, 14, 40, 24,
90, 0, 21, 81, 16, 25,
42, 30, 0, 18, 16, 30,
36, 60, 9, 100, 56

Page 45

1. 28, 48, 46
2. 99, 48, 77
3. 96, 40, 26
   36 plant and animal species

Page 46

1. 252, 196, 296, 102, 156, 320
2. 567, 54, 275, 171, 84, 225
3. 24, 80, 36

Answer Key

Answer Key

Page 48
1. 6,666; 15,705; 8,028
2. 36,856; 15,536; 15,783
3. 21,735; 16,200; 31,750
4. 192 nuts

Page 49
1. 600; 5,600; 3,000; 1,600; 360,000
2. 420; 400; 360; 12,000; 60,000
3. 1,950,000 flowers
4. 450 kinds of orchids

Page 50
1. 2,387; 1,012; 1,023
2. 1,428; 2,332; 1,550
3. 2,400 eggs
4. 276 postcards

Page 51

Page 52
1. $12 \div 3 = 4$ $8 \div 4 = 2$
   $12 \div 4 = 3$ $8 \div 2 = 4$

2. $10 \div 2 = 5$ $18 \div 3 = 6$
   $10 \div 5 = 2$ $18 \div 6 = 3$

3. $12 \div 6 = 2$ $20 \div 5 = 4$
   $12 \div 2 = 6$ $20 \div 4 = 5$

Page 53
1. $56 \div 8 = 7$ $36 \div 4 = 9$ $25 \div 5 = 5$
   $56 \div 7 = 8$ $36 \div 9 = 4$

2. $42 \div 6 = 7$ $24 \div 3 = 8$ $14 \div 2 = 7$
   $42 \div 7 = 6$ $24 \div 8 = 3$ $14 \div 7 = 2$

3. $35 \div 7 = 5$ $72 \div 8 = 9$ $32 \div 4 = 8$
   $35 \div 5 = 7$ $72 \div 9 = 8$ $32 \div 8 = 4$

4. 4 nuts   5. 9 stamps

Page 54
Note: Some possibilities listed.

1. $18 \div 3 = 6$ $81 \div 9 = 9$
   $18 \div 6 = 3$ $81 \div 3 = 27$
   $18 \div 9 = 2$ $81 \div 27 = 3$
   $18 \div 2 = 9$

   $30 \div 5 = 6$ $63 \div 7 = 9$
   $30 \div 6 = 5$ $63 \div 9 = 7$
   $30 \div 3 = 10$ $63 \div 3 = 21$
   $30 \div 10 = 3$ $63 \div 21 = 3$
   $30 \div 2 = 15$
   $30 \div 15 = 2$

   $50 \div 5 = 10$ $45 \div 5 = 9$
   $50 \div 10 = 5$ $45 \div 9 = 5$
   $50 \div 25 = 2$ $45 \div 3 = 15$
   $50 \div 2 = 25$ $45 \div 15 = 3$

2. 8, 4
   6, 4
   5, 6
3. $4 \times 4 = 16$
   $3 \times 9 = 27$
   $5 \times 4 = 20$

Page 55
1. $9\overline{)81}$ = 9 $2\overline{)8}$ = 4

2. $8\overline{)56}$ = 7 $7\overline{)14}$ = 2

3. 8, 7
   7, 10
   10, 7
   1, 8

Page 56
1. 12, 23, 42

Page 57
1. 107, 332
2. 101, 136
   312 miles

Page 58
1. 11 R3, 9 R2, 41 R4
2. 47 R1, 12 R5, 138 R1
3. 99 R3, 205 R2, 102 R2

Page 59
1. 50, 30, 25
2. 9, 75, 12
3. 50, 45, 101
4. 18, 72, 25
5. 60, 25, 50
   corn, chocolate

Page 60
1. $54 \div 9 = 6$
2. 8
   72, 9
3. $291 \div 3 = 97$ or $291 \div 97 = 3$
4. 38, 13
5. 61, 69
6. 163 R3, 100 R3

Page 61
1. 4,350 plants
2. $4.60
3. 19 days
4. 16 snapshots

Page 62
1. $6 \times 5 = 30 \div 3 = 10 \div 2 = 5$
2. $10 \div 5 = 2 \times 4 = 8 \div 2 = 4$
3. $49 \div 7 = 7 \times 6 = 42 \div 6 = 7$
4. $90 \div 10 = 9 \div 3 = 3 \times 6 = 18$